"Wow!" said Henk. "Look at Karim's cool haircut!"

Henk had a number 9 top. He had boots like Karim's too.

He had loads of Karim stuff.

And now Karim had the best haircut ever.

Karim's Haircut

Written by
Jill Atkins

Illustrated by
Alan Brown

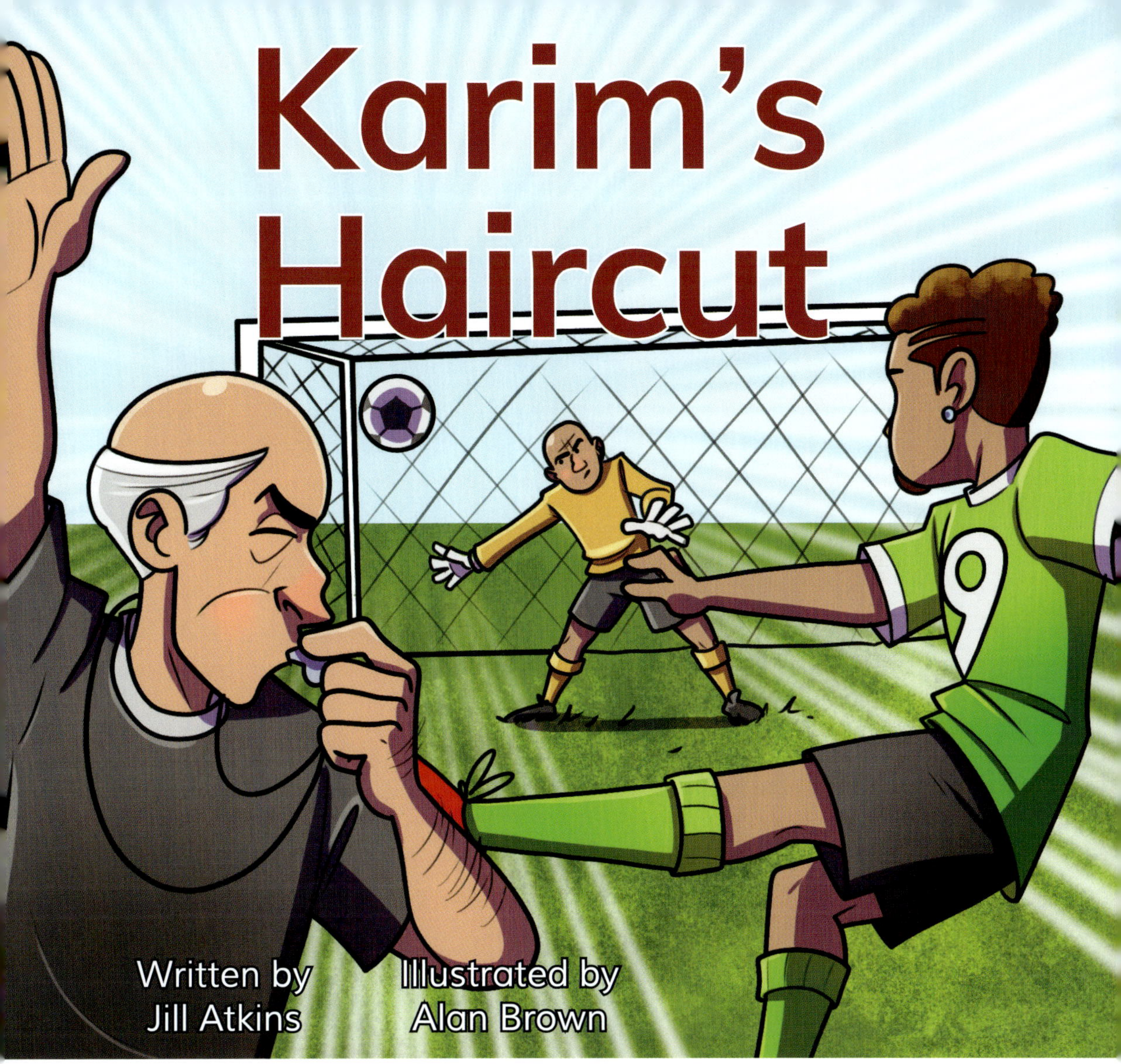

Published in 2026 by
Norwood House Press
2544 Clinton Street
Buffalo, NY 14224

Printed in the United States of America

Library of Congress Cataloging-in-Publication Data:
Names: Atkins, Jill (Children's author). | Brown, Alan, illustrator.
Title: Karim's haircut / written by Jill Atkins, illustrated by Alan Brown. Getting a kick / written by Jill Atkins.
Description: Buffalo, NY : Norwood House Press, 2026. | Series: Phonics all-stars: phase 4
Identifiers: ISBN 9781978578388 (pbk.) | ISBN 9781978578395 (library bound) | ISBN 9781978578401 (ebook)
Subjects: LCSH: Reading--Phonetic method--Juvenile fiction. | English language--Phonetics--Juvenile fiction. | Haircutting--Juvenile fiction. | Hairdressing--Juvenile fiction. | Soccer players--Juvenile fiction. | Extreme sports--Juvenile fiction. | Hobbies--Juvenile fiction.
Classification: LCC LB1573.3 A796 2026 | DDC 372.465--dc23

CPSIA compliance information: Batch #CW26NHP: For further information contact Norwood House Press at 1-800-237-9932.

Henk waited in the crowd with his dad and his little sister.

“Come on, you Greens!” he yelled.

The men in green ran onto the turf.

KARIM
9

At the end, it was three-one to the Greens. Karim got a goal too.

Henk turned to his dad.

"I need a trim like Karim's," he said.

"No," said Dad.

The next morning, Henk felt sick.
He had bad pains in his gut.

They dashed to see the doctor.

It was his appendix!

Henk was sick for three nights.

So he missed the Greens in the cup.

Henk's little sister visited him.

"You missed a good one," she said. "Karim got a hat-trick in the cup."

Henk felt bad he had missed it.

"Look, you have a visitor," his sister said.

Henk sat up with a start. It was Karim!

"You are my number one fan," Karim said to Henk.

"Thank you," said Henk with a big grin.

"Karim seemed a good chap," said Dad. "Shall we pop to see the barber?"

So they did!

Getting a Kick

By Jill Atkins

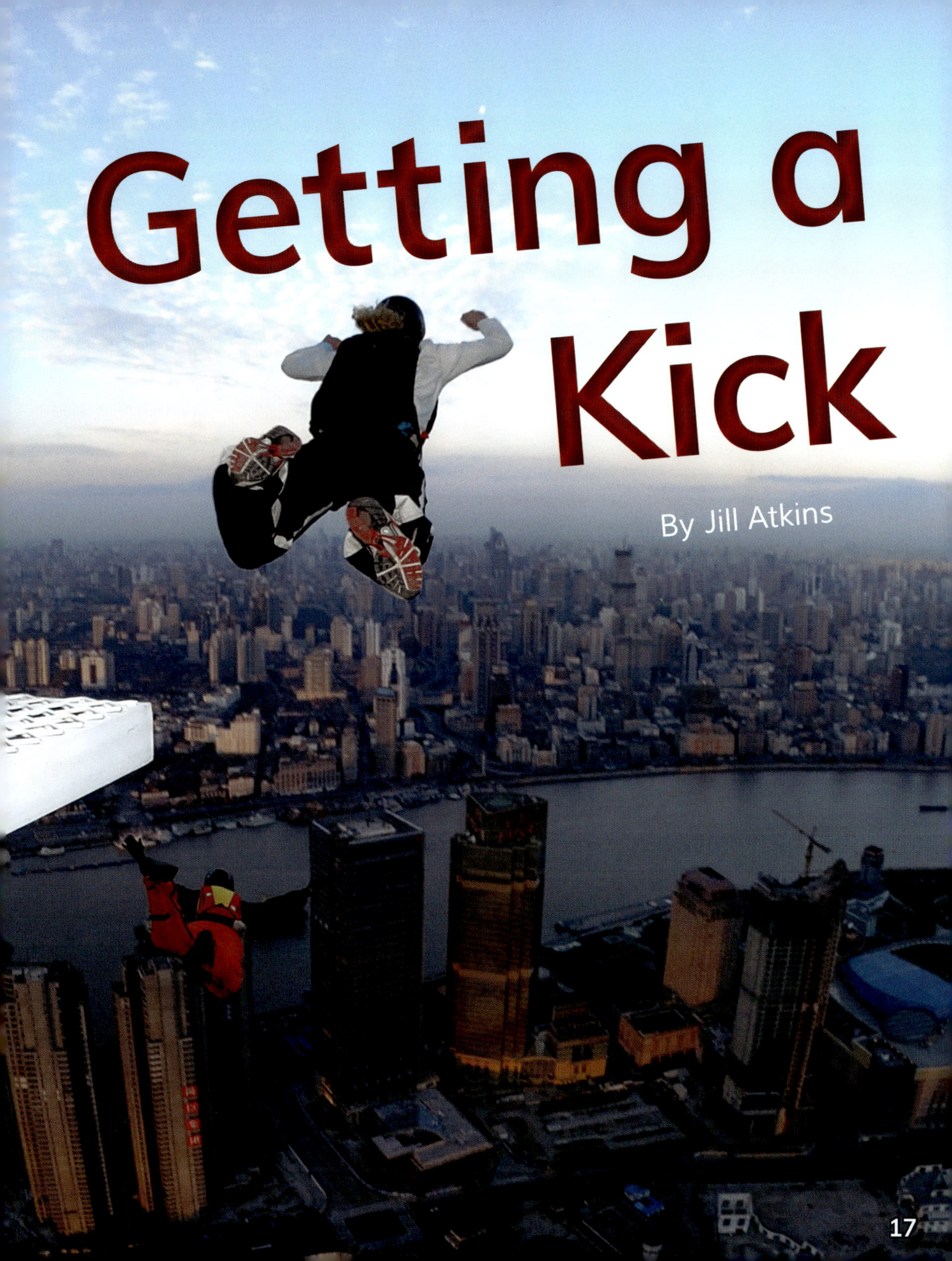

Will you get a kick
out of scoring a goal?

You can train with the lads.

Then it is the big night.

Run, aim, kick and *thwack*
... What a goal!

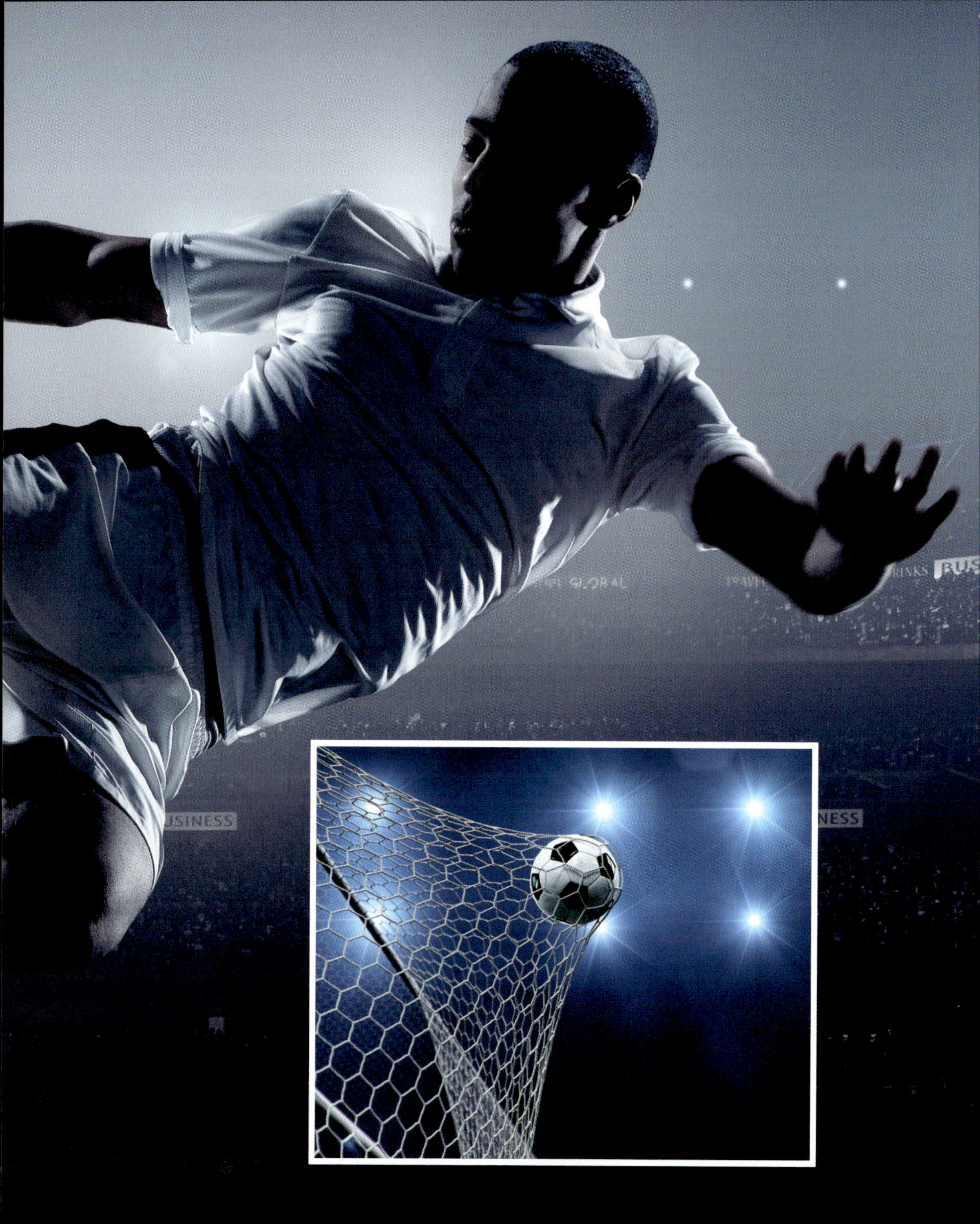

OBJEKT

Will you get a kick when you sail a boat?

A gust of wind might tip the boat up. You will get wet, but you will not be in peril.

Will you get a kick when you swim with sharks?

No, thanks! Some sharks have such sharp teeth.

Will you get a kick out of running?

You might just jog. Or you might run a lot quicker than that.

It will be good when you get to the finish and see the ribbon.

Will you get a kick when you speed down a trail?

You might skid or get stuck in the mud.

Pump the legs, up and down. It is a good habit to have, as it keeps you fit.

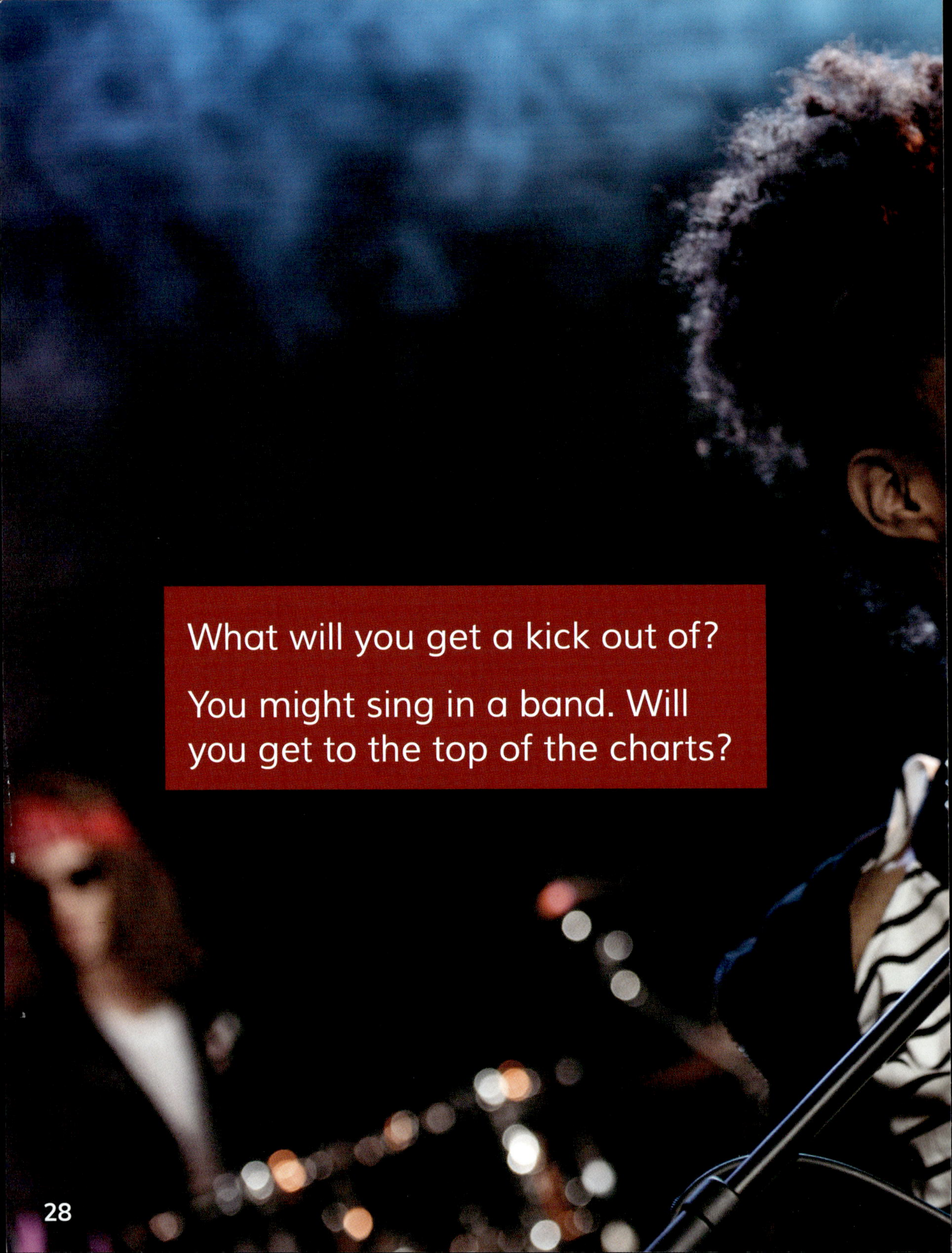

What will you get a kick out of?

You might sing in a band. Will you get to the top of the charts?

Or you might get a kick with painting.

You might like to cook – or potter in the garden.

We all get the best kicks from things we like to do.

What do you like to do best?